This book is due for return on or before the last date shown below.

The GONZO Way

Anita Thompson

Fulcrum Publishing

To Hunter

Library of Congress Cataloging-in-Publication Data

Thompson, Anita.
  The gonzo way : a celebration of Dr. Hunter S. Thompson /
Anita Thompson.
    p. cm.
  ISBN-13: 978-1-55591-622-0 (hardcover :alk. paper)
1. Thompson, Hunter S. I. Title.
  PN4874.T444T46 2007
  070.92--dc22
  [B]

                                    2007016608

Printed in Canada by Friesens Corporation
0 9 8 7 6 5 4 3 2

Design: Jack Lenzo
Editorial: Sam Scinta, Faith Marcovecchio
Cover Art and Graphic Details: Ralph Steadman

Fulcrum Publishing
4690 Table Mountain Drive, Suite 100
Golden, Colorado 80403
800-992-2908 • 303-277-1623
www.fulcrumbooks.com

 Contents

Foreword by Douglas Brinkley 7

Preface 13

Lesson 1: Learning—That's What It's All About 23

Lesson 2: It's Wrong When It Stops Being Fun 37

Lesson 3: Politics Is the Art of Controlling Your Environment 53

Lesson 4: *We* Is the Most Important Word in Politics 63

Lesson 5: Truth Is Easier 80

Lesson 6: Buy the Ticket, Take the Ride 97

Lesson 7: Never Apologize, Never Explain 106

Acknowledgments 108

Honor Roll 111

Foreword

"Do you know where I can find a diamond?" the speedy voice on the line asked me. "I need a really nice diamond—no bullshit—as quickly as possible."

I was used to getting strange telephone calls from Hunter S. Thompson at all hours; nothing unusual there. But his urgency that particular night was disarming. "Slow down, Hunter," I replied. "What are you talking about?" He chuckled, and I could almost see his sly smile. "Well, Dougie," he said, "I'm getting married."

For the past few years Hunter had been dating Anita Bejmuk, and his lust for the younger beauty had turned into love. That much I knew. The pair had met through mutual friends, become acquainted over football-watching Sundays at Owl Farm, and grown ever closer as she ably assumed myriad duties as his editorial assistant. Anita, tall and slim with long blonde hair and fierce brown eyes, was in her early thirties. She evinced a winning humility that belied an indomitable Slavic capacity for suffering. With her rosy cheeks and free-and-easy way, she seemed as ready for mentoring as Hunter was for feminine nurturing. He quickly fell in love with her, and at some point made the mental leap to realizing that she would make a loving wife. Haunted by an inordinate fear of losing Anita to another suitor, and increasingly despondent at the prospect, Hunter got it into his head that a diamond ring would prove the cure-all for his elder man's blues. Convinced that commercial jewelers foisted flawed merchandise upon foolish innocents, Hunter called me that wee morning in the hope that I might know someone in New Orleans who dealt in fine gems on the up-and-up. I did. Before long Hunter was consulting with Keith Miller, an underground jewel merchant, and the rest became history. Flowers, love letters, designer chocolates, and finally the diamond came flooding Anita's way. As beautiful as the ring was— boasting a near-flawless three-carat-plus center stone flanked by a smaller baguette-cut pair in a classic platinum setting Hunter designed himself— the deal-maker proved a love letter so exquisite she simply couldn't turn him down. With his heart pounding wildly, Hunter proposed to Anita on March 22, 2003. They wed a month later, on April 24, 2003, along an alpine stream. Thus did Hunter and Anita become One. For about a year after that they lived in a state of perpetual honeymoon, holing up for long, blissful stays at hotels such as the Carlyle in New York and the Kahala Mandarin

Oriental in Honolulu. Back home, Owl Farm took on a more frenetic, productive, and happy-go-lucky work rhythm. Together the couple brought out his best-selling *Kingdom of Fear*.

In addition to an obvious mutual passion, shared humor, and intellectual respect, much of their relationship was cemented in a bodhisattva-and-acolyte dynamic. Besides working together on a weekly ESPN column, Hunter and Anita exchanged a constant flow of ideas on reincarnation and purgatory and the road ahead. Sometimes it felt as if the Owl Farm parlor had become a Zen den. That may come as a surprise to *Fear and Loathing in Las Vegas* fans who have fixated on the image of Hunter as an acid freak forever in search of another tank of ether. Perhaps such readers have not heard of the Zen Lunatics living in the tall grass behind the ancient tree trunks. Contrary to his popular reputation, Hunter was as much one of those as his own sometime touchstone, Henry Miller.

Don't get me wrong. Hunter wasn't a lotus man per se. He didn't sit cross-legged for hours on end and *ommmm-ommmm*. But once he settled in with his drinks and marijuana—and provided there were no NFL or NBA games to be seen on the big-screen TV—he often turned all flame and fever to philosophy. Somewhere along the line—

perhaps when he moved to New York to work as a copyboy at *Time*—he had read Soren Kierkegaard and Arthur Schopenhauer and Alan Watts, and ever after enjoyed the sport of gorging through their cyclical death-and-resurrection speculations. Crazy detours into erotica—be it *The Story of O* or the *Kama Sutra* or the tawdry monthly *Hustler*—didn't detract from his earnest interest in the variations possible in existence. Fiery planets and faraway stars informed part of his intellectual flirtation with The Unknown, though Hunter rallied against bogus astrologers like a race car out of hell. He was a spiritual seeker after genuine at-oneness, and could sniff out a zodiac charlatan at any range.

Epiphany and catharsis may have been Hunter's goals in holding these philosophical summits at Owl Farm, where saviorism tended to be deemed a human illusion, but I rather think he just liked showing off. Always the consummate journalist, Hunter enjoyed probing other people's spiritual beliefs, because doing so provided him a window on their hidden lives, and thus an advantage over them. Never forget: he was first and foremost a trickster. For all intents and purposes, he had already determined his libertarian rules for living as a teenager in Louisville. But as he aged, he enjoyed sharing the folk wisdom of his experience—which Anita mines in this gemlike book, *The Gonzo Way.*

When Hunter committed suicide in February 2005, Owl Farm's Zen den became a funeral parlor. The Vajra sword was sheathed. No more midnight debates over what was Buddha's face before he was born. No more adrenaline-fueled imaginative floods worthy of Hans Christian Andersen. No more Raoul Duke or Lono or Ray or Wild Man or Hey Rube or Mystic Sufi. And for Anita Thompson, no more husband. The bouncing sunlight in her life was extinguished on that pistol-ripped winter night. Everybody grieves differently. Anita, rather than merely mourning, has lunged into a mission to posthumously honor the great man she married. Along with Hunter's family and closest friends, she saw her husband's ashes fired from a 153-foot silver dagger topped by a clenched red Gonzo fist high into the Rocky Mountain night. Refusing to pity herself, she launched a smart little magazine called *The Woody Creeker*, complete with regular illustrations by Hunter's brilliant collaborator Ralph Steadman. And now she has written *The Gonzo Way* ... for, as Hunter taught her when they first started watching football together, everybody fumbles—it's the recovery that matters. Whether this volume will contribute to Anita's healing or inflame her to learn more about her late husband is yet to be seen. I hope it will lead to both. In any case, I applaud her for seeking the views of some of the people who knew Hunter best and dutifully recording for posterity some of their most cherished thoughts of him.

Anita refuses to let Hunter be remembered in paucity. She touts his literary accomplishments like a town crier, and is ardent to bring what she learned from him to new generations of readers. What you're holding in your hands, my friends, amounts to closure of some sort. Make up your own mind about the enclosed wisdom's merits and usefulness to your own life. But give *The Gonzo Way* a whirl. You've bought the ticket; now take the ride. Dally for a while on the spiritual and political side of the Gonzo philosophy. It just might do you some good—like chicken soup laced with Tabasco, it's soothing and bracing at the same time, just as Hunter would have wanted. It's your doorway into Owl Farm.

—Douglas Brinkley
February 14, 2007
New Orleans

PREFACE

The choice I faced after the shock of losing my husband was whether I was going to be crippled by his death or inspired by his life. What you have in your hands is the manifestation of the effect he had on me, the seven lessons that I have been fortunate enough to learn from him, and that I am willing to pass on. People often ask me, "What was it like being married to Hunter S. Thompson?" And I reply with his own favorite self-description: it was like living with a teenage girl trapped in the body of an elderly dope fiend. Hunter had the energy, the vitality, and the curiosity of a young girl. He also had a depth of wisdom at his disposal that came with his age and experience, and a keener eye than anyone I have met before or since.

Hunter cultivated, carved, sharpened, and polished his life like a fine sparkling diamond. This book is about what I learned from my husband as I watched him craft his life and observe others crafting theirs. It was not always easy living with Hunter, but I bought the ticket and took the ride and have still been riding the wave, and I remain very grateful for those years I spent with him. I was twenty-five years old when we met, and a young twenty-five at that. Hunter knew it and brought me into the loop, and I've never been the same. He turned out to be my best friend, my boss, and my teacher, all in one. He helped me see my own strengths and weaknesses, and taught me to never, ever try to be like anybody else—especially Hunter S. Thompson. Perhaps the most important lesson I learned from him was this: play hard, work hard, but always be yourself.

If you are one of those who loved the Hunter S. Thompson Show for its decadence, its crazy debauchery on every level, mixed with Wild Turkey, Dunhills, and multitudes of uppers and downers and screamers and laughers and high-speed car rides with the top down hovering on the edge for the adrenaline rush, and if you are one of those people who assume those sorts of things alone will enable you to live the Gonzo Way, this book is not for you. If you are one of those people who just needs a few guns and bombs and a loaded pipe of hashish, and friendships be damned, this book is not for you either.

There is a difference between the image in Hunter's works on your bookshelf and his true life-style, which developed a life of its own in the skewed public eye. Yes, Hunter's greatest work of art was his own life. And those aforementioned scenarios, with all their speed, substances, and forays to the edge, were indeed part of his life, and certainly interesting. But they were hardly his whole story, and they may not be what you're about at all, nor should you strive for them either. Hunter often said that he never advocated drugs, alcohol, and craziness as a way of life for anyone else, although they certainly worked for him. But there was so much more to him, too, and not everyone grasps that.

My good fortune in crossing paths with Hunter has opened many psychological doors for me and opened my eyes to the senses of humor and possibility that lie in even the most twisted of scenarios. That is why I want to share with you some of his basic wisdom, the wisdom he lived by. Analysis of his literary and journalistic legacies, legacies that will last long after all of us reading this are dead, is for another book. This volume is geared toward the other aspect of his legacy: you, Hunter's readers, and particularly those of you who are interested in living up to your unique potential in individual style with the vigor and curiosity and courage to fight for your beliefs and for your neighbors well into old age. I know when I'm not living the Gonzo Way—it's usually when I'm tired, or start to worry about what others expect of me or what they think of me, and the fear sets in. But it takes me only a few moments to remember the things that Hunter taught me, to reread a passage or two, and then I am calm and grateful again. The Gonzo Way is an attitude rather than a set of rules. These seven lessons came in handy for me when I faced a life without my beloved and times were very dark and I was afraid for my future. But no. I had the Gonzo Way as a guide. And I use it every day of my life now. With these lessons, it is as if Hunter has been walking with me through my troubles and victories since his death. Learn, be with the tribe, never be afraid if you have loved ones on your side. Never take yourself too seriously, and always find some fun, in any situation. Respect yourself and your tribe, and you will live the Gonzo Way.

This book is geared toward the younger readers with whom I have developed a relationship over the last few years since Hunter died. Most careful readers of any age understand that although he was indeed the embodiment of sex, drugs, and rock 'n' roll, that was not actually Hunter's essence. His essence is what enabled him to maintain his free-spirited attitude and still earn a living. And he not only earned a living, but he also developed a legacy that I believe will remain intact long after the rest of us, and our grandchildren, are gone.

The Castle

… Jesus! What's happening in this world?

What indeed? The bag-boy grinned. The desk clerk grinned. And the cop crowd eyed me nervously. They had just been blown off the track by a style of freak they'd never seen before. I left them there to ponder it, fuming and bitching at the gates of some castle they would never enter.

—Hunter S. Thompson, Rolling Stone #96,
November 25, 1971

One night, while Hunter was sleeping, I read the *Rolling Stone* magazine version of *Fear and Loathing in Las Vegas*, because I loved the book and earlier that evening he had mentioned that there had been "almost nothing" edited out of the magazine copy when he compiled the book manuscript. The word "almost" inspired me to search for *more* of the story. As it turned out, the paragraph above was the only part omitted. I wrote out the seven sentences on a piece of white paper and taped it to the refrigerator. The next day Hunter was happy to find the long-lost paragraph, but he didn't give me an explanation of why it had been deleted. And that's okay.

There are so many things he didn't actually explain to me. And I'm still searching for answers. So are you, I suppose—that's why you're reading this book. The only answers I can give you are the ones that apply to me. I don't profess to know everything there is to know about Hunter S. Thompson; nobody does. But I'm happy to tell you what I learned, what I saw, and what I am still seeing inside those gates as I keep trying to reach the castle.

The castle? That is the term I am going to use now, for lack of a better one, to wrap my mind around what was so special about my husband's life philosophy, his work, and what remains so unique in his legacy: his attitude.

When Hunter and I first met, it wasn't always obvious to me which of us was younger. It was like encountering a child prodigy: a cigarette-smoking, whiskey-drinking child prodigy. He was not child-ish, but childlike. He loved toys—we called them his props—things like screaming hammers, explod-ing pens, powders that within seconds could turn your drink into glue, and electric beer cans that sent shock waves shooting through the bodies of those star-crossed enough to be picked for a prank. But beyond his jokes and his pranks, the quality that really distinguished Hunter was his attitude that anything is possible, that any situation can be turned into fun and then put on a page to add to the greatest masterpiece of all: a remarkable life.

To see your life clearly, to live it like a champion, not taking abuse from anyone, you have to develop your own set of rules, just as Hunter developed his own set of rules for writing. The rules he crafted for living worked too—like a charm. As his fellow literary genius Oscar Wilde once put it in words that apply to both of them: "Do you want to know the great drama of my life? It's that I have put my genius into my life; all I've put into my works is my talent."

Riding the Crest of a High and Beautiful Wave

Hunter was funny, sexy, wickedly smart, and a very powerful teacher. Yes, by meeting him I had been blown off the track by a style of freak I'd never seen before. But I was lucky. He didn't leave me there to ponder it, fuming and bitching at the gates of this castle I would never enter. No, he took me storming into it with him, riding a high and beautiful wave that would crest over the last years of his life.

As I write this it's been two years since Hunter died. During the first year, I wrote letters to him every day, trying to make sense of the loss. Because I was terrified to lose contact with him, I'd write about everything I could remember. On a daily and nightly basis, I also let my memory scan every square inch of his body. I was afraid that somehow, over time, the memories would fade, and I would forget. Would I forget his voice, the low mumble when he'd wake up, the staccato sound of him talking on the phone to one of his many long-distance friends, the chuckling, the yelling, the whooping? Would I forget how he smelled, that combination of Chanel No. 5 and Old Spice that mixed with his own chemistry into a scent so wonderful to me?

The unfortunate truth of losing a loved one is that, yes, those memories fade. But something interesting also happens: we begin to learn more about ourselves. What I have learned from Hunter's loss is how to be both stronger and more flexible at the same time. For so much of my personal growth, my sense of humor and sense of self, I do in fact have Hunter to thank, because he was a relentless teacher, and I'm so grateful for all that he taught me.

As if on cue, as some of those physical memories start to fade, Hunter's essence and what he offered to me as a partner and a student have become sharper and more crystalline, especially when I need that wisdom most. That is what I want to share with you. I was pretty young when I met Hunter; I'm older now, and continue to feel ever more blessed with his spirit, in life as well as death.

Just what is it that makes Hunter S. Thompson so interesting in the long term? What kind of person and writer is it who could inspire such a range of readers—from PhD candidates around the world to *Playboy* bunnies to thirteen-year-old sports fanatics to presidents of the United States—to admire and even seek to mimic his work?

When Hunter died, no less than a onetime Leader of the Free World, his friend Jimmy Carter, wrote to me that it is really the legacy of so vast a range of people that Hunter's work touched that would bring me comfort after Hunter's death. And he was right.

So what is so special about Hunter? His writing? His snow-leopard-like network of lifelong friends? His uncanny ability to stumble out of the house and shoot three clay pigeons in a row or hit a propane-bomb bull's-eye from fifty yards out? Those talents and distinctions remain fascinating to me, but the quality that still intrigues me the most about Hunter is his life philosophy, as it were. We can use this wisdom of his as a guidebook—not to write like him, because that is impossible, and not to drink or smoke like him, as that too is impossible, not to mention inadvisable, but to live our own lives to the fullest, using Hunter S. Thompson as your guide to living the Gonzo Way. His attitude, his spirit, and his essence will live forever in his work, and through those of us who paid attention and try to pass on what he taught us.

LESSON 1

Learning—That's What It's All About

If You Don't Know, Come to Learn … If You Know, Come to Teach.

—Motto on the invitation to the National District Attorneys' Convention in Las Vegas, April 25–29, 1971

What was it like being married to a teenage girl in the body of an elderly dope fiend? It was fun. What was it like being married to one of the seminal writers of our time? It was an education. Hunter had the experience, the insight, and the wisdom that come with age, but he also had the enthusiasm, the vitality, and the curiosity of a teenager. He never stopped wondering about things, and that is what kept him young. He never stopped learning.

In fact, he made the aggressive pursuit of learning a cornerstone of his life as well as his career. We all know that Hunter was an amazing writer. That's because he learned to be an amazing writer. He made a conscious effort to study everything from the Bible's book of Revelation to the outlaw motorcycle gang that provided the subject matter for his first book. Hunter was twenty-nine years old when he wrote *Hell's Angels*. To do so, he set about studying every aspect of the biker phenomenon in addition to riding with the Angels for a full year. He spent six months writing the first half of the book, which forms the scholarly and methodical part of the story of the social and political phenomenon that was the Hell's Angels. Then one day he looked at the calendar, and it occurred to him that he had four days to complete the entire second half of the manuscript! But instead of panicking, he rented a hotel room on the outskirts of San Francisco, loaded in a supply of Dexedrine and Wild Turkey, and finished the book. Smart people agree that the second half is by far the better—the part that kicked off his career. But they also acknowledge that the story wouldn't be nearly as compelling without the careful context in which it was framed. Don't be one of those unthinking people who believe that it was the drugs and alcohol that produced the wild Gonzo attitude in the second half of Hunter's groundbreaking first book. Here is the secret: *Hell's Angels* owes its genre-busting success to the previous fifteen years Hunter had spent studying the art and craft of writing. Remember that Hunter had read many of the classics of literature by the time he turned eighteen. Yes, there was a time when he was notorious for cutting classes, but while he was cutting classes and being a delinquent, he was also reading Plato's "Allegory of the Cave" and every word of the daily *Louisville Courier-Journal*, his hometown newspaper. Then he would spend the rest of the night *writing*. It didn't matter to him if he was writing an article or a love letter to a beautiful girl. And if he didn't have a letter or story to write, he would copy pages out of F. Scott Fitzgerald or Ernest Hemingway to "feel the rhythm" of their prose. The most important thing for him was to learn his craft—from the masters.

That is how he could stay up for four days and four nights and produce one of the best books on American sociology in recent history. Hunter explained to me one night that it was his "muscle memory"—having those early years of practice—that enabled him to pull it off.

Hunter rode with the Hell's Angels simply in order to understand them so he could write their story as fully and accurately as possible. He had no intention of joining the biker gang. He simply wanted to observe them—to learn. What Hunter and his friend and contemporary Tom Wolfe had in common was their ability not only to engage themselves in a story, but to engage themselves utterly in learning more about whatever story they were pursuing. "He was doing what I thought was the way to write. What he did was very much what I did," Mr. Wolfe recalled. "He really went to see things, and more than that, he joined in. And with the Hell's Angels, that's not a small undertaking."

Finding the "Rock in Your Sock"

Writing was what Hunter called the "rock in his sock," the one thing that he had as a tool, but also as a weapon. It doesn't cost much, you just put a huge rock in a large white sock and swing it around. People will leave you alone, and you will also have the confidence of having a serious weapon.

Writing was the one thing Hunter could do better than anyone around him, and as such the one thing he knew he could earn money at. He tried other jobs, including an attempt at barber school, in case the "writing thing didn't pan out," in San Francisco. Later, he would wake up at four o'clock in the morning to stand in the employment line, hoping to be picked for day-labor jobs. When he couldn't even get hired for those, he realized that writing was his only hope, and that he'd better work hard to learn the craft so he could pull it off.

So he set himself to learning to write. And when he chose to put his meticulously acquired literary abilities to journalism, he made a point of backing up his immense talent with scrupulous research and genuine scholarship. Hunter was an intensely curious individual even as a child, and he remained that way his entire life. Anything that was interesting to him launched him on a passionate quest to seek more information about it—aggressively and nonstop.

One of Hunter's long-standing go-to resources was his friend and editor Shelby Sadler, who worked with him on many of his books and articles. I remember so many wee-hour phone calls for research assistance to the onetime Republican speechwriter's apartment-cum-library outside Washington, D.C. A particular favorite, she recalled, began "Shelby? Hunter. Tell me everything you know about the Rape of Nanking." She revealed, "It's a good thing I could always distract him with political chitchat for a few minutes while I scrambled around in my vast reference collection for whatever it was Hunter wanted at any given 4 A.M. I'll never know if he actually thought I knew everything I pretended to rattle off the top of my head to impress him.

"Of course," added Shelby, who first met Hunter in 1986 when she commissioned an article from him as senior editor of the short-lived *IQ Magazine*, "perhaps my proudest moment as his abstruse-research specialist came one night in 1989, when I really did know off the top of my head that the primary symptom of the very rare black hairy tongue disease he was inquiring about is 'elongated filiform papillae,' and within ten minutes of his call faxed him clinical photos of the afflicted tongues of three different sufferers thereof.

"It blew Hunter away," she laughed, "and for months after that he'd phone four or five times a night and pepper me with increasingly arcane queries in every imaginable subject area—chemistry, physics, poetry, history, you name it—just to see what other bizarre stuff I could come up with that he might be able to use someplace. It got exhausting, but it sure was fun, mostly because we both learned a lot we'd never have picked up otherwise." Shelby admiringly summed up his lust for learning: "What few people realize is that smart was cool to Hunter, and he was never the least bit ashamed to admit it."

Not only did Hunter choose curious and intelligent friends, but stupid people didn't last long in his life. Stupid, like drunk, was unacceptable to him—people who loved to learn, like Shelby and others, always had a special place in Hunter's heart, and had a special place in his work.

Of course, not all of Hunter's research was of the typically scholarly variety. He threw himself equally enthusiastically into other subjects of interest too. He was particularly interested in women, for example, which probably comes as no surprise to anyone who knows a bit of Hunter's history. He loved women. As a boy, he studied their habits. "Anything pretty girls did was fascinating to me," he said to me in May of 2002. He would watch them giggle and talk in the hallways between classes at school. He talked to them, read about them, and fell in love more or less constantly. He also read women writers, such as Anaïs Nin and Ayn Rand, in order to better understand how smart women thought.

Hunter knew the difference between love and sex, and the combination of the two became a driving factor in his craving for knowledge about the world around him. It was in the mid-1980s that he became night manager of the famous O'Farrell Theater in San Francisco, "the Carnegie Hall of Public Sex in America," as he liked to call it. He studied all sides of the sex world, from the high art of *The Story of O* to the raunchy, B-grade XXX trash you can find in any adult dime store's 75-

percent-off bin. He spent two years researching "feminist pornography" and interviewed hundreds of people across the sex industry. The result is another aspect of his learning that paid off in his life. Hunter always had smart, good-looking girlfriends. He was suave.

As his fellow reporter Laura Palmer remembered of her first encounter with Hunter in South Vietnam in August 1974, "I'd been in Saigon about a week when Hunter Thompson arrived at the Continental Hotel. His presence sent sparks through the mostly male members of the press corps. Hunter was their alter ego, the person many fantasized they would be if they didn't have wives, children, and mortgages. He was the harmonic convergence of sex, drugs, and rock and roll. A rebel without a cause but with plenty of charisma.

"I watched the late night frenzy around him in the hotel garden, sure his arrival meant I'd publish nothing in *Rolling Stone*. It took me a week to work up the courage to introduce myself, but once I did, we began working together. I knew how to cover the story and helped Hunter get organized enough to work. The surprise was how astute his journalistic instincts were."[1]

---

[1] Laura Palmer, *War Torn: Stories of War from the Women Reporters Who Covered Vietnam* (New York: Random House, 2002).

Never Throw Anything Away

Despite his wild-man image, Hunter was also an utterly professional journalist, and as such was a remarkably fastidious record keeper. One of his dearest friends, the late *60 Minutes* correspondent Ed Bradley, reflected admiringly on Hunter's devotion to his own journalistic files and their usefulness in his later work. "I don't know if he stumbled into or delved into this treasure trove of everything he ever wrote or that anyone ever wrote about him in his life," Ed recalled. "In the last years of his life he was, in many ways, recycling material because it was material previously written by him and others. But recycling in a unique way, and I think that is the renaissance [in Hunter's work]. You look back at what he wrote then and what others wrote to him and the way he chronicled those things," Ed continued. "It's amazing—he had stuff from high school. He never threw anything away. I sit back now and I think, jeez, I wish I had kept all of those notebooks. I'm thinking of stories that I did in the sixties when I was working in local radio, my first jobs. Boy, I wish I had kept those scripts.

"How did he have the foresight to keep everything he ever owned? *The Rum Diary*, for example: *The Rum Diary* manuscript sat in a drawer in my kitchen for a year. When his brother died, he messed around and it was too late for him to catch a flight to Louisville to be there in time for the funeral. The only way he could get there was to charter, and he needed to borrow some money. He asked me for the money and I said, 'Well, when are you going to pay me back?' And he gave me a date and I said, 'Okay, I'll write you a check.' And he said, 'Well, I'll give you some collateral.' I said, 'Your word is collateral; I don't need anything.' He said, 'No, no, take this,' and he fished in a drawer and handed me an envelope, and I took it and stuck it in the kitchen drawer. It was in there for a year and a half, and he paid me back when he said he was going to pay me back. But *The Rum Diary* manuscript was just sitting there; we both forgot about it. And then one day he asked me about it and I dug it out—and it was *The Rum Diary*, ready to publish. That he could have this thing all of those years later, it just speaks volumes about Hunter. I thought it was just amazing."

I got my own taste of that aspect of Hunter on my first night of Real Work for him, in the winter of 1999, which consisted of photocopying letters for possible inclusion in *Fear and Loathing in America*, the second volume of Hunter's correspondence. Professor Douglas Brinkley had extracted them from the vast archive of some thousand boxes Hunter had amassed in his Owl Farm basement. Doug would scour through the boxes and turn sideways the letters to be potentially included in the manuscript, which, in its electronic form, was later to be known as "the disk." My job for that evening was not so much to read the letters, but to photocopy them so that Doug could take the copies to his assistants at the University of New Orleans, where they would be transcribed onto a computer disk. After that, the entire assemblage would be read several more times by historians like Doug Brinkley who would edit out the superfluous ones and draft notes explaining the context of the letters selected for inclusion in the book.

Hunter and I had been friends for two years at this point. I would come by Owl Farm with my friend Don to watch football. I didn't know anything about the sport, but was curious and wanted to learn. What was so wonderful about football that it could make weekend, and often lifelong, buddies of men who often seemed to have nothing else in common? I wanted to know, and was invited to learn about the game from the master.

Bet with Your Brain, Not with Your Heart

Hunter taught me about football by forcing me to bet on it. We would place house bets of $20 on the final score. The real betting action, however, took place during the course of the games themselves. Every play was a betting opportunity: Would Peyton Manning's next play be a pass or a handoff? Would the Colts make the fourth down? That's how he taught me, and that's what I call learning in action.

In addition to learning the rules and strategies of the game, I learned to bet with my brain rather than bet on the team I wanted to win. Hunter always said that was the key to betting successfully, but it only sank in for me after many painful losses.

After a game was over, Hunter would often ask me or someone else present to read out loud. We would have discussions about the news or enjoy a chapter from one of his books. It was fun. He once showed the assemblage a video that he and Emmy Award–winning filmmaker Wayne Ewing were working on and asked us to give it a grade of A+, A, A-, B, C, D, or F. He was serious. Hunter truly wanted to know our opinions and to learn why each of us felt the way we did.

This night, however, marked the first time I was actually being paid to help him, so I acted accordingly and did what I was told. He needed the help because his assistant had recently fled and his secretary at the time was not accustomed to engaging in the creative side of his work. A team of long-time friends and colleagues filled the kitchen when I arrived: Curtis and the late Donna Robinson of the *Roaring Fork Sunday* newspaper, Wayne Ewing (who would later create the documentaries *Breakfast with Hunter* and *When I Die*), along with several other long-standing friends, such as Gayle Golding from Aspen, all gathered around him under a massive storyboard he had covered with photographs, quotes, letters, notes, and clippings.

Hunter presided over the evening wearing a blue-and-white-striped shirt, legs propped up on the counter, head tilted back with a cigarette dangling in its holder from between his lips, looking handsome as ever. The group was conceptualizing and debating, sometimes angrily, which letters should be included in the second collection and which burned. At one point, when one of his favorite letters was about to be axed, Curtis took the stand like a lawyer defending a client.

I watched with fascination. As all this was going on, the secretary ushered me into another room to get me started on my work—the reason I was there, of course. She showed me how to operate the Xerox machine and handed me a few boxes. I got the thing fired up and started the process. The action continued in the other room, though not as clearly over the hum of the copier. Suddenly, Hunter's deep shriek came through loud and clear: "What do you mean, she's photocopying in the other room? Get her in here! She needs to learn this stuff!" Some vague arguing ensued over the fact that these letters needed to be copied so that the deadline could be met. Hunter had priorities, came the consensus, so within no time at all we found ourselves lugging the massive photocopier into the kitchen, and I continued to do as I was told—to photocopy. But more important … I was there to learn.

LESSON 2

It's Wrong When It Stops Being Fun

Hunter was fun. He never stopped playing and seeing the undercurrents of humor in every situation, weird or not. If a room was getting too boring, mundane, or just plain predictable, Hunter would come roaring in with some unexpected blast of fun. It would arrive in many forms, such as smashing a cane to bits in front of 1,100 fans in line to see him at the Barnes & Noble bookstore in New York's Times Square, or pouring a pitcher of ice water on an unsuspecting college crowd at a university-sponsored talk, or, heck, setting loose a lunatic wearing Hunter's own press pass on a serious Democratic presidential candidate's train, as Hunter described the great "Boohoo" incident of Edmund Muskie's 1972 whistle-stop campaign tour. Of course, Hunter's antics weren't always so dramatic. Sometimes it was just a matter of putting on lipstick during a serious editorial meeting.

What was it about Hunter's thinking that made him so much fun to be around? It was largely the conscious efforts he made: he wanted to be fun, as well as have fun.

He would try anything once, he always said, but if it was not bringing something to the table, like a laugh or a decent story to retell in his work, it was wrong. Life, if it is to be lived with grace and in the Gonzo Way, must be filled with courage, truth, love, and laughter. It was very simple with Hunter: when these elements faded, his humor ended, so he had to start the day over. And he often did—he'd just go back to bed and try again.

Correspondent Ed Bradley believed that Hunter's love of fun stands among his most important legacies. As Ed told me from his home in Woody Creek not long before he died in the autumn of 2006: "His legacy is also the many memories that all of us have who had Hunter in our lives. I can remember getting up in the morning and [my wife] Patricia would see that there was a stuffed lamb and a snake on the front porch. And she'd say, 'What is it, what is it?' And I said, 'You know Hunter was here.'

"That bird over there [on the shelf]—you push the button and it squawks. That's another Hunter gift, you know. There's a can up here somewhere— it's a propane tank that has a bullet hole in it, which is a souvenir of one of my shooting exhibits with Hunter when I hit the bull's-eye on the propane and it blew up. You have all of those memories, and

Hunter also railed against the system, and I guess that's part of his legacy."

Never a Dull Moment

Hunter founded what he called the Too Much Fun Club. The Too Much Fun Club is the nexus that cemented his friendship with so many of those who shared his love of literature, journalism, history, language, sports, and the highest-stake sport ever, politics. The club consisted of excellent minds and people who loved to do their best work but always remembered to have fun. One member was Terry McDonell, Hunter's longtime friend, who remembers that "in the end, the best moments were the shockers of his open humanity, his smile when he knew you were getting the joke." When Stacey

If it's true that a man can be judged by his friends and his enemies, then I feel pretty good.

Hadash, one of Hunter's political advisors and dear friends who started in politics under James Carville during the Clinton campaign, got engaged to Terry, Hunter "took credit for us being together and told us he'd be at our wedding dead or alive. We got married on December 3, 2005, and he was." The wedding was magical, overlooking the Hudson River on a crystal-clear evening with a vibrant sense of fun in the air. I remember their wedding fondly, and agree that Hunter whooped it up all night long with us.

Terry remembered the night of the first memorial service we gave for Hunter at the Jerome Hotel in Aspen, Colorado, on March 5, 2005. "I have a photograph of myself speaking at the first memorial service, the one in town in early March. I have lipstick on. Behind me is a huge cutout of Hunter. Everyone in the room who knew that particular joke is laughing."

Indeed. Hunter made people laugh when he was alive and is still making us laugh after his death. I believe that's why he resonates with so many young, and young-at-heart, people, such as his intellectual-property lawyer and late-night phone friend George Tobia of Boston. Most of their business dealings took place between the hours of midnight and 5 A.M. But it wasn't all serious business. During my first few years with Hunter, I knew George only from these phone calls. Now I think it is appropriate, in the pages of this book, in this chapter, for me to reveal a secret. This respectable Boston attorney was also a main supplier for one of Hunter's addictions. George indeed supplied Hunter, often via unmarked overnight FedEx boxes, with "things." What were these things? Let me list a few that came in a package dated August 14, 2002:

Full-Speed Crazy Roach	Magic Hammer
Rat-on-a-Leash	Horror Axe
Exploding Lighter	Severed Foot
Exploding Pack of Gum	Dagger with Retractable Blade
Shocking Lighter	Jelly Beans (with projectile snake)
Shocking Beer Can	Mixed Nuts (with projectile snake)
Shocking Calculator	

The list goes on, and the packages came at regular intervals. Hunter explained that this type of "equipment" was needed to ratchet up the element of fear in his "experiments" on people. He wanted every box of supplies to be bigger, weirder, and meaner, so as to facilitate his efforts to "scare the shit out of many cool people." He was indeed a game master and a connoisseur of fine toys. Some of my fondest memories with Hunter are from those days, when the lipstick was applied to the accompaniment of good music and he got out some weird toys, or, as he called them, props.

Hunter also gained quite a bit of joy from another favorite type of prop: guns. As even his casual readers know, Hunter loved guns. I learned to love guns as well. One activity during his courtship with me consisted of us going outside and target practicing, blowing up these magnificent propane canisters that would light up the whole sky, not to mention lighting up your whole fight-or-flight gland! I have no interest in going into great detail about guns in this book, or any other book for that matter, but it goes without saying that they were a part of his life. His longtime neighbor and good friend Gayle Golding, who helped him on many projects over the years, explained that a lot of the fun of being around him came out of Hunter's "natural sense of entertaining."

"He sure loved to entertain," Gayle remembered. "He was hands down the most fun of all the friends I have ever had. Hunter's house was the modern-day salon, where ideas and laughs flowed among friends in the kitchen and there was never a dull moment." Gayle fondly recalled the first time he taught her how to shoot: "First, we drove behind the Woody Creek Tavern looking for a keg to put in the backyard field to shoot at. We finally found one and took it back to Owl Farm. Then we took several two-inch nitroglycerine targets, the exploding kind, and attached them to a small propane canister, and boom!—it would explode fifteen feet up in the air.

We'd each take turns shooting. Anytime you were frustrated with your accuracy, he would hand you a shotgun. He wanted everyone to feel like a sharp-shooter—and boy, he was fun!" Gayle proved on many occasions to be one of the true friends Hunter knew he could trust to handle both his most serious and his most hilarious times at Owl Farm.

Fire in the Nuts

Hunter's love of fun and games and "experiments" also shot through his writing and gave it the unique style his late reporter pal Bill Cardoso dubbed "Gonzo." Tom Wolfe called Hunter "the greatest comic writer of the twentieth century. And that's not a small thing. I also compared him to Mark Twain."

He explained that Hunter wrote in a style and about things that people hadn't seen before, but at the same time, and like another great American humorist, let his fantasies run wild. "It's a very American thing," Mr. Wolfe told me. "Twain's first short story that brought him fame was 'The Celebrated Jumping Frog of Calaveras County,' [which] introduced readers to a life of miners in the West that most people had no idea about, but at the same time it was a fantastic story about a champion jumping frog who had been made to swallow BBs so he couldn't jump very well. You knew that somehow there was a lot of embroidery, but you didn't care. He did both things: introduce you to something real and new and, at the same time, a flight of fantasy. That's what Mark Twain did over and over again. If you read some things like *Innocents Abroad*, *Life on the Mississippi*, and those things, he's constantly doing that."

And that's exactly what Hunter did in his life as well as in his writing: take us on a surreal, twisted journey. Tom Wolfe agreed, which is why, he said, he especially loved Hunter's June 1970 *Scanlan's Monthly* article "The Kentucky Derby Is Decadent and Depraved." In fact, he readily admitted that at times he has used Hunter's writing to inspire his own: "I would read Hunter the way I read Henry Miller, which was when I was getting stale and the words were just coming up flat. I would read Henry Miller or Hunter, and it was like putting carbonation in your brain. And you felt like, 'Hey, I'm back to life. I can actually write this thing!' That's what I remember. By that time, I was probably too deep into my own mannerisms [to obviously reflect Hunter's influence on his style]. Besides, he was inimitable."

And fun—always fun, in a characteristically smart sense. As the lead character in *Fear and*

Loathing: On the Campaign Trail '72, Democratic presidential candidate George McGovern recalled some thirty years after he first met Hunter: "Whenever I would think of him, I would start to smile. Playing in a restaurant or in a bar, coming up the aisle of the campaign plane, ambling along, not looking at anybody in particular, sometimes scowling, I would start smiling because I knew he was going to say things that twist, and usually he made a good point and I thought his questions made good points. And then, at the end, if I would ask him something, he'd say exactly what he was thinking."

I asked Senator McGovern how important he felt it was during the 1972 campaign to maintain a sense of fun. He agreed that keeping a sense of humor, especially in such a high-stakes endeavor, was critical—certainly to keeping Hunter interested in the political scene. There's no doubt in my own mind that one of the elements of campaign journalism that most captivated Hunter, that turned him on to politics for life, was the possibilities it opened for him to make connections and develop a network with people in a field filled with not just excitement, but just plain fun. Speaking of Hunter's fondness for jokes and pranks, Senator McGovern added: "Those were the things that made me develop a deep and lasting affection for him. ... That only added to the interest that I had in what makes him do this and what makes him say that. And from the beginning, I never had a boring moment with Hunter. I never had a trite question from him, and he always kept his own counsel."

Which Side Are You On?

Douglas Brinkley, one of Hunter's best friends as well as his authorized biographer, has their relationship to thank for the fateful day he decided to inject more fun, excitement, and integrity into his own life. Doug was at a signing in Florida for his first solo book, *The Majic Bus*. He had already met Hunter and had spent a good bit of time on the phone with him while he and his students were crisscrossing the country on the Majic Bus to visit places of historical and literary interest, including Owl Farm.

At the signing party in Florida, Doug recalled, "Everybody was so pretentious, and I had some gin and tonics and I remember wishing Hunter was there because he was a bull that carried his own china shop around with him, and if he was at that party there would be some action and he would have popped the bubble of hypocrisy that was going on." That night, Doug went back to his hotel room and asked himself: "Which side are you on? I'd rather be on Hunter's side than this. This is not why I'm interested in books and publishing. Not for this sort of horrible, pretentious atmosphere. So I looked around and decided, 'I'm going to Hunter's.'"

That same night he called Owl Farm and said, "Yeah, I'll come out." Instead of dragging on with his dull and pompous book-signing gig, Doug there and then committed to working with Hunter on editing the first volume of his mentor's letters, *The Proud Highway*.

Meeting the Champion of Fun

In retrospect, Doug Brinkley regarded his commitment to having more fun as a pretty easy, and definitely wise, decision. He had found it awfully fun to be around Hunter from the moment they met, when he first brought twenty-seven students on two Majic Buses to Owl Farm to a warm and generous welcome from the Champion of Fun. "I did not know him," Doug recalled, "but we went and stopped at the Woody Creek Tavern on our way to Alaska. We went up to Owl Farm that night, and what struck me was that on this road trip we were meeting great American writers, people like Toni Morrison, who we thought would be great because she had won the Nobel Prize, but she was all about herself and wasn't very generous—but with Hunter it was so exciting, because he loved the kids. He was shooting a gun through their books and opening up food he had gotten for them from the Tavern. He was being a host, being funny and grabbing their cameras and filming them instead of them filming him, and he was in a very good mood about it all.

"At that point I remember he said to me, which was the basic thing: 'This is very good.' He liked that I had anarchy going on, but it was controlled. It was anarchistic, but in the bubble. It wasn't all over the place." But it was definitely fun—for Doug, for the students, and especially for Hunter.

Doug remembered Hunter fondly as a Peter Pan figure in his life as well as in his writing. "He always wanted to be kind of a fountain of youth, in the sense that a lot of people of his generation said we all had to grow up and get these nine-to-five jobs, and Hunter continued to be our youthful conscience. He kept that rock 'n' roll youth attitude alive; he continued to embrace it, and they, in turn, embraced him."

Forever Young

Why do young people embrace Hunter so enthusiastically? And why do the young-at-heart embrace him? "Because Hunter was forever young," said

Lynn Goldsmith, a dear friend and photographer who has been photographing and documenting the rock and roll movement in America since the early 1960s. Subjects of her work include everyone from Bob Dylan and Mick Jagger to Michael Jackson and Deepak Chopra. She first started photographing Hunter in the mid-seventies. "That was his state of mind. He means so much to so many people young or old because he was able to express his inner child. Often someone who is not as wise does not have the gift to express that side of themselves. We're all kind of young at heart, and people forget that. He reminds you of who you really are—the part of you that is forever young."

Doug agreed: "When you're young and you have attitude—when you're traveling, you're struggling, hitchhiking, you're riding motorcycles or you're doing drugs or you're drinking too much—the students all knew Hunter had done all that. And they knew that he probably outdid them at it all, so it gave him a kind of hyperyouth status, and he responded to it. And oddly, it's true. He had a kind of tolerance for the mistakes of young people because he could see how clearly they were going down a wrong path, but he understood that that was part of what life was, being young, and he didn't mind. He didn't hold it against them."

Where Were You When the Fun Stopped?

But Hunter was not, of course, only about fun and games. His serious side proved equally important in his life and work, and he pointedly refused to ignore his responsibilities as a member of American society. Hunter had a painfully clear idea of what the American dream really entailed: contributing to the betterment of the world, whether doing so seemed like a lot of fun or just a lot of hard work. He was far too smart to even think about trying to laugh away the world's real problems.

Another of Hunter's closest friends, longtime Pitkin County sheriff Bob Braudis, recalled the last year of the twentieth century as a particularly harsh time for his old pal in Woody Creek. "We were continually talking about how depressing national politics were [in the autumn of 2000]," Bob said. The night of George W. Bush's first election, for example, was hard on Hunter. "It was almost bedtime," Bob continued, "and we thought that Bush had lost and Al Gore had won, and then all of a sudden one of the national news channels started flashing the results from a couple of states like Florida. Those people who had made the projections that Gore had won were eventually proven wrong, and it was like sticking a needle in a balloon in the kitchen. There was something going on, and it was just me and Hunter that night, and we were looking at each other as if to say, 'This is not good.' And, yeah, we were depressed. But Hunter, like I, separated depression into clinical depression and logical depression. Logical depression is saying, 'Shit just happened; that is so sad; we should be depressed. We're depressed because there's an asshole in the White House.' That's logical depression, and you recover from that. You recover from that very quickly."

Bob went on: "Hunter was not a crossbearer. He didn't suffer and moan and whine for long. He recovered. The recovery is very important. I could tell when Hunter was getting depressed. You could try your best to cheer him up; usually, though, what he needed was just a little time and reflection. If you're depressed for more than a couple of days, you've got to do something about it—and usually just a couple of days later Hunter would be impish again, and he would have a new crusade. He was, in a way, very Zen."

What Hunter was not was very accepting. He was certainly not complacent when he didn't like the way things were going. To the contrary, he was a fighter: a Zen warrior, if you will. "I really do believe that the reelection of George W. Bush in '04 really depressed him," Bob Braudis recalled, "because he would say, 'Where were you when the fun stopped back in 2000?' I think that by '04 he really felt that, not just of his personal fun, but America's. Characters like Gary Hart in the U.S. Senate—they don't exist anymore. It's over, that fun of politics on a grassroots level, at a high level. Today it exists in little subterranean pockets, but I think that Hunter started seeing the America of 2000, Y2K until '05, was an America that did not feel like he wanted it to be. He was embarrassed by it."

And if Hunter was not having fun, or could not at least see the potential for fun, he knew it was wrong. There is no doubt in my mind that the deteriorating political scene ushered in at the close of 2000 depressed Hunter to the end. Whenever the good side was winning, he and his fellow snow leopards would be out working, and fun would be had by all. For Hunter didn't just have fun in his personal and professional life; he saw the ultimate fun in politics.

LESSON 3

Politics Is the Art of Controlling Your Environment

I don't want to be a product of my environment. I want my environment to be a product of me.

—*Jack Nicholson in* The Departed

Hunter titled his book about Bill Clinton's 1992 presidential campaign *Better Than Sex* to underline what he felt about politics: pure passion. Although he would at times laugh and admit that of course it's not true that politics is better than sex, the point wasn't always that clear. Hunter did truly love politics, and it was largely because he found politics so much fun.

But why did he feel that way? Politics certainly isn't always fun, and at times can be pure agony—but if you stick with it, and if you do it right, you just might win. And winning is nearly always fun. What makes Hunter's passion for politics so fascinating is that his side lost so much more often than it won, and he had just as much fun with it anyway.

Politics crept into almost all of Hunter's writing, particularly his sports writing, for as he always said, "Politics is the ultimate blood sport." Ed Bradley said with great fondness that Hunter's columns for ESPN.com often had far more to do with politics than sports, despite the pleas of his editors at the sports network's Web site. Hunter may have written more in the last five years of his life than he had in the previous fifteen because he loved to write the ESPN column so much. After all, he had begun his career as a sportswriter at Florida's Eglin Air Force Base in the late 1950s, so it was natural for him to end his career doing the same thing he had loved all his life: writing about sports. In fact, his last published piece was for ESPN: an article about playing "shotgun golf" with actor Bill Murray. Even when Hunter wasn't officially writing a sports column, he would sneak the subject into his texts. His columns for the *San Francisco Examiner* as its "media critic" in the 1980s and '90s, for example, were full of sports. Whether Hunter was covering games for the base paper or for ESPN, as Ed Bradley remarked from his home in Woody Creek in the winter of 2005, "He used sports, which was so important in his life, as a point of departure for politics and things of interest to all of us. He was just masterful in the way that he was able to do that in those ESPN columns. And I also think that things like the Gonzo Papers were, in so many ways, a reflection on our time."

Part of what made Hunter's political journalism so compelling was that he infused it with the same passion he put into his sportswriting. Former U.S. senator from Colorado Gary Hart remembered the first time he and Hunter met, which was of course through politics. It was in 1972, during the Florida primary. "Word got around that Hunter Thompson was there," Senator Hart explained. "As you well know, throughout his life he was at least as fascinating to other journalists as he was to the public at large. Journalists were just mesmerized by him, so even at that time, there was a buzz in the press corps that was following McGovern and Eagleton in the primary that Hunter Thompson was there. I didn't even know what he looked like, and then the famous Boohoo incident occurred on the Muskie train, and the question was 'Who was the Boohoo?' and the forum continued as to who that might be. And then I think we bumped into each other in a hotel, and I think we had a talk, if not an interview, at that time. I think he was trying to figure out 'What's going on here? Who's McGovern? Who are you guys?'—and you could not *not* like him. He was amusing; he was interesting; he was different. And then it just followed from there.

"There were all kinds of incidents along the

way," Senator Hart chuckled. "I remember ending up in California when the movie *Easy Rider* had just come out—we were staying at the Wilshire Hyatt House in L.A., the McGovern campaign, and Hunter was there, and he said, 'What are you going to do when all this is over?' And I said, 'I want to go in search of America.' He said, 'Okay, come downstairs,' so we went downstairs and he said, 'I got the bike for you.' That was the famous Vincent Black Shadow. He had it in the courtyard, and it was an object of amazement to people, because it was huge. I mean it looked like a small horse. He wanted me to get on it and he'd take me outside of Los Angeles. He claimed that the day before he had had it going 105 miles per hour. The mythology had already been created, largely by Hunter himself, that he was taking all kinds of controlled substances, and I thought, 'Well, now, the last thing you'd want to do is get on a bike.'

"He told me afterward that it was the second largest bike ever built in the world. It's famous. The reporters would go down there and look at this thing because it looked like a Shetland pony," Senator Hart laughed. And the reason the other journalists found him so interesting, he added, was that "it was fun to be Hunter. That's the reason why so many of them tried to be like him—because it's fun. Hunter had the knack for making politics accessible and understandable to people. Well, certainly for young people over the years—a generation and a half. He made it interesting, fun, lively, dramatic, sometimes overly dramatic. And people could say, 'Oh, my God, is that what's really going on?' It was like peeking behind the curtains of politics in general. He made it very accessible. He clearly had this unique style, and people loved to read what he wrote."

I asked Gary Hart if he knew of any writers today who are making politics accessible.

"No one comes even close," he replied. "He had impact. What he did is, he was so amazing to other journalists, and he was a cult figure, so I think they all wanted to be Hunter Thompson. They didn't like writing. They were not excited about writing standard prose and turning it in to these editors who were from another generation and didn't want little Hunter Thompsons. They'd send it back to them and say, 'Write this the way you were taught in journalism school.' But the reporters all wanted to be Hunter. They wanted to be able to write like that; they wanted to be able to get it in print. So there were a lot of aspirants. I think there is a generation or so of journalists out there who grew up reading Hunter and trying in some way or other to be Hunter." Not one of them, of course, succeeded.

At the Top of the Mountain, We Are All Snow Leopards

The man Gary Hart worked for in 1972, George McGovern, appreciated another quality in Hunter that his fellow journalists may not have. "He probably disagreed with a lot of the things that I did," Senator McGovern recalled, "but we at least had a high respect for each other. You know, there's something else that people didn't always grasp in either Hunter or me: we were both bedrock patriots. Some of the young people were so angry about the American war in Vietnam that they almost turned against America, but we never did that. Neither one of us had any desire to live in Switzerland or Sweden or France or anywhere else. With all of its faults, which are many, and with all of its blunders, which are huge, I think both of us will go to our graves thinking we live in the greatest country on earth. And what we were trying to do is live up to the enduring values of the nation."

Senator McGovern added, "I know [Hunter] liked that campaign slogan of mine: 'Come Home, America.' And people interpreted that as a call for isolationism and not as a call for America to come home. He was a bedrock patriot."

As the great western writer Edward Abbey once described his own political passion, "I know my own nation best. That's why I despise it the most.

And know and love my own people too, the swine. I'm a patriot. A dangerous man." Those words apply equally, of course, to Hunter. He loved his country for all its flaws, and hated it for the same reason. That's why he focused so much of his writing and thinking on what he called "The Death of the American Dream." Much of Hunter's life and work was fixated on the death of the American dream. The high-water mark where the wave broke and rolled back. The sixties, when the people joined in a fight they believed they could win. That they were being heard was crushed by, among other things, the tragic events of 1968. The death of Martin Luther King Jr., Bobby Kennedy, and the government-sponsored violence around Chicago. Hunter was as important a defender of the republic as any senator or statesman. He was a bedrock patriot and loved his people. He knew the potential that we as a country had, and the realization that we were not living up to that potential was very painful. When Hunter felt pain, he liked to share it.

Hunter spent the rest of his political-writing career looking for someone with George McGovern's principles who might be able to win all the way to the White House. He never found that candidate, but he never stopped looking. And it's our job to continue the search.

All Politics Is Local

Hunter had made a pitch to become his own ideal candidate by running for sheriff of Pitkin County in 1970. He had no intention of actually *being* the sheriff; he simply wanted to make a statement. And he sure did. Although that bid failed, forever after he acted as a major force in his own community's politics, including as one of the founders of the Woody Creek Caucus, in which I make a point to remain active. After all, it's up to every one of us to speak out for the interests of the places we call

> We are all politicians. The only difference is that some of us are winning, some are losing.

home. As fellow Woody Creeker Ed Bradley put it, "We need the Woody Creek Caucus and caucuses all over this country to make our voices heard, and I think that what the Woody Creek Caucus says and does, whether it's heard or not, is important. I think it's whatever your belief is. Whatever your political beliefs are, it's the system to express yourself—express those beliefs, and if you're opposed to the system, to rail against the system. That's the American, and that was Hunter's, way, and that's the Woody Creek way."

The Woody Creek way, indeed. If politics is the art of controlling your environment, and all politics is local, then it certainly makes sense to start at home. Wizards have said since the beginning of time that home is where the heart is. No matter how far Hunter's politics took him out of Woody Creek, his heart remained at home, which even inspired the formation of a new type of community and a new way of life rarely heard of outside the beatnik cowboy Shangri-la that is Woody Creek.

George Stranahan, the noted physicist and founder of the Aspen Center for Physics as well as the Roaring Fork Valley's COMPASS educational system, the Flying Dog Brewery, and Stranahan's Colorado Whiskey—among myriad other philan-thropic pursuits—had a vision when he bought all the acres then available in Woody Creek with his friend Bob Craig in the early 1960s. George had an interesting idea: he would sell the land to people he liked, and knowing that few of those people could afford the land at full price, he would sell it to them for 50 or 60 percent below market value. He would do so under one condition: that if they ever sold it, they would have to give George the first right to refuse it at 50 or 60 percent of the current market value. He didn't want people in the neighborhood who were in the real-estate business. The boom-ing industry that was soon to take over and nearly destroy the local housing and living environment in Aspen was not welcome in Woody Creek, and George made that clear. A perfect resident for the scene he and Bob Craig were building in Woody Creek was Hunter S. Thompson. Although Hunter didn't have the money, he sure had the wisdom, the weirdness, and the attitude to contribute mightily to the community. "One of the things that Hunter established in Woody Creek, which is still a sort of Utopia," George explained, "is that you can be as weird as you want in Woody Creek and you will be as accepted as a straight person." Hunter contributed to that character for forty years, and that legacy continues to this day.

LESSON 4

We Is the Most Important Word in Politics

If "politics is the art of controlling your environment," then Hunter was certainly a political master. But he didn't achieve that mastery alone. In fact, many people seem surprised that Hunter did not believe the most important thing in politics is winning. Victory was simply one of the more fun aspects of the ultimate game. To him, an even more important part of politics came in the friendships one could make along the way. Even better than that was the chance to devise strategy and tactics and gamble on them in the highest stakes sport of all.

Early in his relationship with Hunter, Doug Brinkley accompanied the press corps to Haiti to cover former president Jimmy Carter's election-monitoring trip to the war-torn Caribbean nation. Because Carter had accorded him exclusive access for the purposes of Doug's book-in-progress on Carter's post-presidential career, at several meetings he and Doug were the only Americans in attendance. Doug said, "I was very happy about that access, and I called Hunter from Haiti to tell him, but he said, 'Oh, no, you're in a danger zone.

You're the only one?' And I said, 'Hunter, I thought you'd be proud of me. I thought that was good.' He said, 'Oh, no … you've got to win one of the other reporters over so that there are two of you with the access rather than just you—so the others are the ones with the problem, not you being totally alone. But if you're the only one … you just can't do that.'

"So the next day I found a writer from *Esquire* in the press pool and I lobbied to get him access with me, and it worked. Suddenly, we were the two—and this was a seasoned reporter—saying, 'What's wrong with those other turkeys? We were able to get in.' And it worked. So I would get advice from him that was practical."

To go it alone was never advice Hunter gave to anyone trying to control his or her environment.

During the 2004 presidential campaign, Doug Brinkley wrote a book about John Kerry's Vietnam experiences, and of course wanted the Democratic candidate to win. When Kerry lost the election, Hunter reminded Doug that the most valuable part of the experience would turn out to be the friends Doug had made along the way. He explained to Doug how McGovern's loss in 1972 had enabled Hunter to make some very good friends who would remain so for the rest of Hunter's life.

Hunter understood the value of friendship

and of the usefulness of friendships in developing a powerful team to work toward a goal. Hunter said and wrote this on so many occasions that it became a household understanding: that "*We* is the most important word in politics." It's a lesson he taught me very, very well—and that brings me to the story of young Lisl Auman.

You Can Beat City Hall

It was in January of 2001. Hunter and I were sitting in the kitchen. It was a typical breakfast, which meant it was about two o'clock in the afternoon. The skies were clear, and Hunter was peaceful. I had already placed his breakfast in front of him, which at that time of year consisted of corned-beef hash and eggs with coleslaw on the side. Next to that was his bowl of fruit (I don't think I was making him his famous gin jello yet); a large Chivas Regal scotch and water on the rocks; hot, sweet black coffee in his favorite lobster mug; fresh-squeezed orange juice; and toast. In a small bowl would have been warm salsa to top his eggs after he had dressed them with just the right amount of salt and pepper from the electric spice grinder. The Sony TV was set to CNN or the History Channel, as always; it was only shut off to be cleaned or serviced or for a new one to be installed. He had already read the *USA Today* sports and national news sections. *The New York Times* would be next.

If it looked interesting at any given breakfast time, he would read his mail. That day, he looked at a letter bearing the return address of a federal women's prison in Cañon City, Colorado. He recognized the name: Lisl Auman. He looked up at me and said something about this being one hell of a crooked case. He had been following Lisl's plight in the papers and on Denver's TV stations the year before and remembered the press reporting that she was not even near the scene of the crime that she had been convicted for. But he hadn't heard much about it since. He turned down the volume on the TV to read her letter, which caught my attention. Without saying anything, he then handed the letter to me. It was a sweet missive in which Lisl didn't ask Hunter for help, as most of the other letters Hunter received from inmates did. She was simply thanking him for the laughs he had provided her. She had read *Fear and Loathing in Las Vegas* while she was in jail, and it had cracked her up so much that she wanted to read his other books. But now that she was in prison, she didn't have access to them because they were banned from the prison library. She concluded, "That sucks."

Hunter explained to me that he had followed her trial while it was being covered by the Denver press and that she had gotten a rotten deal and didn't belong in prison. Hunter knew the Denver Police Department and could spot corruption a mile away. He was quiet for a while before he called Hal Haddon, his lead attorney and friend of thirty years. Hal and Hunter both hailed from that tribe that began forming in 1968 following the assassinations of Bobby Kennedy and Martin Luther King Jr. and that summer's government-sponsored violence at the Democratic National Convention in Chicago. Hal was serving as Gary Hart's campaign manager when he and Hunter finally met in 1974, after which they went on to share a long legacy of political victories and defeats.

While Hunter sat in his catbird seat that morning pondering whether he, not just as a journalist but as a political activist, wanted to take on the case of this innocent girl sitting behind bars for her supposed role in the death of a police officer, he had to take into consideration more than just himself. That morning, so early in my relationship with Hunter, marked one of the most valuable lessons I have ever learned, and that is that *we* is the most important word in politics.

Hunter sat there already knowing that I would

back him. Lisl Auman's plight was something that I understood in my heart was special and needed my support. When Hunter was working on any vital project, I was by his side. But Hunter needed more than just our newly assembled two-person team based out of the Owl Farm kitchen, so within minutes he called Hal Haddon.

"Counselor?" he barked. "It's Hunter. I have to talk to you about a case, about a girl who wrote to me from prison: Lisl Auman. Do you know about her?"

"Oh, yes, she really got a raw deal," Hal replied.

"Should we go for it?"

Hal gave the green light.

From that moment on, Hunter opened the floodgates for his closest friends and allies to join forces for the "Free Lisl" campaign. Within two weeks, he had a team of lawyers from all over the country working on her behalf: Gerald Goldstein from San Antonio, Texas, as well as Aspen; Michael Stepanian from San Francisco; Abe Hutt and Rachel Bellis from Denver; George Tobia from Boston; Keith Stroup from Washington, D.C.; Gerald Lefcourt from New York; and Morris Dees from Atlanta. Norm Mueller, on behalf of the National Association of Criminal Defense Lawyers, and Rachel Bellis wrote an amicus brief, a document intended as a "friend of the court" opinion as to how the judges might approach Lisl's appeal.

Up until this point, a respected public defender named Kathleen Lord had been handling the appeals process and doing a wonderful job on the legal side of it, but she was working more or less alone, through the Colorado Public Defenders office. Although it is one of the best public defenders offices in the country, with a solid reputation thanks to some of the original lawyers who opened and set the tone for the operation in 1970, Colorado public defenders typically have a crushing workload, and the office lacks the resources or experience to manage a media campaign like the one mounted by the Denver Police Department against Lisl. A media campaign on that level can change the public perception—and legal standing—of a person unfairly trapped in the system's web. So Hunter felt it was his job as a journalist to bring Lisl's case to the court of public opinion, which tries cases in the newspapers as well as on TV, radio, and the Internet, and, ultimately, in people's hearts and minds, and would play a vital role later when the district attorney would be faced with the decision of whether or not to reprosecute Lisl.

Before Hunter mustered his army of supporters, according to public opinion Lisl was a bad apple and seemed clearly guilty as an accessory to the slaying of a Denver police officer. News reports claimed that she had not cooperated with the police and that she was the girlfriend of the skinhead who had pulled the trigger. Neither was true. Yet according to the polls, 75 percent of the Denver public believed Lisl Auman was guilty of killing a police officer, an unfounded reputation based on the skewed bias of the local press establishment and the organizing efforts of the Denver Police Department to shine an ugly light on her—so as not to shine the light instead on their handling of the tragedy that day.

Hunter understood the system. He had been involved with the courts even as a child, but more important, he had memories of how to beat that system, memories going back to the age of nine when FBI agents came to his house to deal with the infamous mailbox incident he described in *Kingdom of Fear* (see Lesson 6: "Would You Do It Again?"). He also knew the first line of defense: the front line of the criminal justice system is held by the criminal defense lawyers. It is no secret that Hunter was a great connoisseur of lawyers. Those are the people he gathered first after his call to Hal Haddon. With these legal wizards at work to free Lisl and give Hunter the background of the arcane felony murder statute, and with others such as Rachel Bellis and Norm Mueller writing the amicus brief to be delivered in time to the Supreme Court, Hunter was free to handle the sparkling Fourth Estate, the turf he had claimed so many years before: the court of public opinion—The Press.

Hunter had a simple strategy to win this campaign: *we.* As I sit here tonight by the fireplace at Owl Farm where Hunter assembled the first group of lawyers on Super Bowl Sunday to bring them into the fight, the memories of the ensuing five years of meetings, briefings, arguments, fears, agony, suspicions, and many, many long-distance phone calls come flooding back. Hunter was in a position in his life to start calling in favors long owed. Some people were called back with a smile, while others were called in via his help-me-or-else tone.

Believe me, it was not always fun. In addition to the high creativity and camaraderie involved, there were also many nights of fighting: agonizing over strategy and the winnability of Lisl's case, arguments with those who discouraged Hunter from working on a campaign that was bringing in no money as well as with those who worried that antagonizing the already hostile Denver Police Department would prove a self-inflicted curse. There were as many opinions as there were players.

What Is the Desired Effect?

"What is the desired effect?" is a question that Hunter often asked when making any important decision. The desired effect here, the effect he wanted to have on his environment in this case, was to free this innocent girl from prison, thereby proving to the world that you *can* beat city hall. The line attributed to Edmund Burke that "The only thing necessary for the triumph of evil is for good men to do nothing" tolled like a tocsin throughout Hunter's entire campaign. The beauty of doing the right thing is that you have more of a chance to forge the crucial *we* behind a cause—the team.

Hunter didn't choose weak friends; weak or stupid people didn't last long in the kitchen (and if they did, they usually turned to wine). He presided over a sterling network of people spanning the country and even the Atlantic Ocean for this cause. So as I sit by the fireplace six years later, I am looking at a map that Hunter drew for me one night that shows the various angles of the public campaign he had set in motion for Lisl. It is a hand-drawn map of the United States. At the center, in the Colorado Rockies, is the kitchen, a large black dot approximately 150 miles from Cañon City. From there the lines spin out like a web to San Francisco, Los

Angeles, Austin, New Orleans, Atlanta, Chicago, Washington, D.C., New York City, Boston, even off the map page to Kent, England's, Ralph Steadman. One of Hunter's last projects with his dear friend and Gonzo cohort was the *Vanity Fair* article Hunter wrote with Mark Seal about Lisl, which Ralph Steadman illustrated.

The list of people at the ends of the spokes was impressive indeed: lawyers from fifty states working pro bono, law enforcement officers, journalists, screenwriters, movie stars, and rock 'n' roll musicians. The Hollywood crowd added sparkle to the campaign: well-known names such as Jack Nicholson, Johnny Depp, Anjelica Huston, Woody Harrelson, and many more. Sean Penn and Benicio Del Toro were the most involved among the Hollywood crowd. Benicio researched Lisl's case and Sean kept constant tabs on her progress, even waiting by the phone the morning the Supreme Court handed down its decision. The Hollywood names are what brought much of the initial interest from the casual citizens scanning the evening news and pricking up their ears at the sound of movie-star monikers, not to mention those of world-class music figures such as Jimmy Buffett and Warren Zevon. Hunter understood his audience: in the court of public opinion, winning requires skill, but it sure doesn't hurt to have the glitzy imprimatur of the top flight of celebrity.

These high-profile figures from the legal, music, and film worlds still constituted only one portion of the picture. Hunter called in the rest of the army over the course of a few months. Hunter's media connections reached far and wide from the very start. After we did a substantial amount of research into Lisl's case, I read two four-inch-thick binders of raw court transcripts and watched six hours of police interviews, and the more we read, the more shocked and horrified Hunter and I grew about the conditions under which Lisl was expected to stand trial. It was, as Hunter called it, a kangaroo court. As soon as Hunter felt he knew enough to start making his views public, he announced his intentions to get involved in Lisl's case in his ESPN column, where he included a link to Lisl's Web site. Colleen Auerbach, Lisl's mother, who had been monitoring the site's hits for the previous few years, said that up until that date, very few people had visited the Web site. Then one day she noticed that the view counter indicated that 150,000 people had logged on to Lisl's site in a single morning. She thought something was wrong with the counter and called the Web technician. No, nothing was wrong; all these people were linking to Lisl's site because of a column on the ESPN.com Web site, a column by a guy named Hunter S. Thompson. Thus did that day mark the beginning of the über-*we* in the "*We* is the most important word in politics" lesson. *We* also includes *readers*! Within three years, Hunter would bring millions more people to read about the case, not just through ESPN and the various other newspapers that followed Hunter's lead, but through the *Vanity Fair* article he wrote with Mark Seal and had illustrated by Ralph Steadman, which was a massive success.

It was the early press on Hunter's work for Lisl that piqued the interest of Matt Moseley, a young and energetic public relations expert who contacted Hunter after he had read an article by *Rocky Mountain News* reporter Jeff Kass, who broke the story of Hunter's involvement in the Lisl Auman case. Jeff remained one of Hunter's main press contacts throughout the entire campaign. Matt Moseley suggested to Hunter the idea of holding a rally on the Capitol steps in Denver on the day that Kathleen Lord would be submitting the appeal brief to the Colorado Court of Appeals. Hunter agreed and quickly summoned his son and many of his friends to help show a united front at the rally.

When Warren Zevon flew in from Los Angeles, Doug Brinkley from New Orleans, Timothy Ferris from San Francisco, and 300 local citizens gathered with signs proclaiming their intentions to support Lisl, the tide turned for her public image. Finally, thanks to Hunter and his friends, plus the new friends he made on the Capitol steps that day, the news was showing a different and more accurate face of Lisl. She did not kill the police officer, and because of Hunter, more and more people were learning the truth.

It's the Recovery That Matters

In Lisl's case, the web that Hunter wove across the country and around the globe acted as a safety net when things seemed to be falling apart at times. When the appeals court refused to overturn Lisl's conviction

> Warriors don't apologize.

several months after the rally, for example, some spirits were dashed. But with so many professional and strong legal minds on board, it took only a few phone calls for Hunter and my confidence to grow strong again.

One added benefit to Hunter's campaign to free Lisl was the friendship that Lisl and I cultivated while she was in prison, during those dark days when she found herself staring out from a tiny crack in the windowless wall of her cell and facing a whole world that seemed to be against her. She was a victim, and she had reached a very low point in her life. Nobody would have blamed her if she decided to live the life of a victim for the rest of her days, suffering the injustice that had been done to her. But she proved to be a fighter, and she had a learned ability to recover. It was almost as if Hunter instinctively knew this about her from the start. That is an understanding that Hunter lived with, told me about, and showed me many times: tight ends in football fumble all the time; it's the recovery that matters. And today, Lisl has recovered fully and is on her way up to the top.

We confronted so many setbacks in this campaign that at times it seemed impossible to prevail. Combined with the constant waiting and worrying, there were Hunter's (and my) health problems to deal with. He had recovered from major spinal surgery and a broken leg, forcing him to relearn to walk *twice* in one year and still earn a living. I've never met anyone with a more profound ability to heal than Hunter. What we didn't know before the operation was that when you have work done to your spinal canal, the messages the brain sends to the body are completely rerouted, in this case, causing Hunter not only to have to learn to walk again, but to write again as well. But he did it beautifully, as always.

My own subtle health crisis came from several years of intense, self-inflicted stress that triggered a thyroid deficiency, which I am just recovering from four years later. I'm well enough now to continue the work Hunter and I started together, finish school, and, yep, write this book. Around the time these health issues were going on, we heard that the appeals court would not reconsider Lisl's case. This meant that her lawyer, Kathleen Lord, would have to bring it before the Supreme Court. Which of course brought its own amount of stress. But setbacks, tragedies, and pain are part of life. It is the recovery that matters.

Two weeks after Hunter died, the Supreme Court overturned Lisl's conviction. The wizards in the legal community, including Gerry Goldstein, the constitutional lawyer who fought alongside Hunter in her case, and others, believed beyond a reasonable doubt that Lisl and the rest of us— *we*—have Hunter to thank. Being a witness and participant throughout the entire campaign, I noticed that a consistent theme ran through it all like a bright red thread. All of our discussions, all the meetings, every phone call, and every word that Hunter wrote were stitched together with his natural Gonzo law, that "*We* is the most important word in politics."

Indeed. The distinguished gentlemen and -women Hunter assembled each played a crucial role in the success of my husband's campaign for Lisl. On that bittersweet day after Hunter's death when I hosted Hal, Gerry, and Hunter's son at Owl Farm to hear the news of the Supreme Court's decision, it felt, in a word, incredible. I'll forever be grateful to have been by Hunter's side through such a magical and righteous fight.

LESSON 5

Truth Is Easier

From the fool's gold mouthpiece
The hollow horn plays wasted words
Proves to warn
That he not busy being born
Is busy dying.

—Bob Dylan, "It's Alright, Ma
(I'm Only Bleeding)," 1965

I thought I knew everything there was to know about my husband until I started talking with Ralph Steadman, the celebrated British artist whose illustrations added so much to so many of Hunter's works. Ralph and I became very good buddies after Hunter died, and he helped enormously to get me through those extremely difficult times, especially during that first year. I didn't know if there was a point to any of my work anymore without my man there to see it. Those days were awful. But Ralph whipped me into shape and reminded me that it is indeed the recovery that matters—that life may well be full of doom and desolation, but we owe it to ourselves and our loved ones not to fall down the well ... but if we do fall down the well, at least to make sure it's a well in the realm of mermaids, not of gloom. And he was right.

One day, in the course of one of our frequent correspondences, Ralph told me something I hadn't known before about his extraordinary relationship with my husband. The inspiration for what he wrote me that day was a quote I had put on my blog from Hunter's beloved book of Revelation. With his characteristic wit, Ralph joked that Hunter "hadn't even heard of the Bible before I met him. ... He realized when he met me just where the wisdom was coming from, but to his credit, he made it his own. It spoke of doom and desolation and enabled him to back his voice, which was and is *original*! He didn't like to say that he loved humanity, but the book of Revelation gave him courage to speak his *truth*—and that was so important to him—without losing face, as though he were an S.O.B. He wanted to sound like an S.O.B., but with humor. Revelation gave him the way." Ralph was, as usual, spot on.

Just How Weird Can You Stand It, Brother, Before Your Love Will Crack?

Any way you can get to the truth, even if it is the truth you fear most, the book of Revelation makes for a good place to start. It's particularly useful when you want to spark up the working vocabulary in your brain: that last book of the King James Bible offers some of the best writing in the English language, according to Hunter. He needed magnificent language at the tip of his tongue to be able to stay true to what he was thinking and get it down accurately on the page. As Hunter put it so beautifully in his Author's Note to *Generation of Swine*: "I have stolen more quotes

> I've been plagiarizing my whole life. It's called learning.

and thoughts and purely elegant little starbursts of writing from the book of Revelation than anything else in the English language—and it is not because I am a biblical scholar, or because of any religious faith, but because I love the wild power of the language and the purity of the madness that governs it and makes it music."

Sometimes that language would be put to producing great writing; sometimes he would use it in rough wordplay on his closest of friends; and on occasion he would unleash it to berate his loved ones outright. One thing that kept Hunter's friends loyal to him, no matter what field they worked in, be it journalism, politics, publishing, Hollywood, avant-garde art, sports, or even finance, was his complete honesty with them. The list goes on of friends who loved Hunter for decades, who worked for and with him over many years despite being sometimes utterly brutalized by him—myself included. We put up with it, and even treasured it, because we all knew that Hunter was just being honest about how he felt at the moment. Often his harshness was meant as a joke, but the jokes always stemmed from a deeper truth. Then a moment would go by and he would appear with a wink and a firecracker as if nothing had happened. It was, in a word, bizarre, but more important, it was honest. That is not something you can expect from everyone you meet.

I was recently asked in an interview about the major discrepancy between the sweet and the cruel Hunter. I was asked what tied those two Hunters together. I answered, "Oh, that's simple. It's honesty."

Ralph remembers the effect that honesty had on him. As he explained it to me, Hunter "knew I was strange, 'a matted-haired geek with string warts' bucking the trend, but also conventional, innocent, and true. Most friends tried to be like him—but not *me*. From a foreign land, I had not met his like and therefore acted accordingly, with respect, until, you know, as with a dog, it will not bite. I think our relationship was based on that— our mutual respect. So he knew I could take his coruscating insults and interpret them as *love*."

Ralph used the same keen artist's eye to see the world around Hunter as he did to see the subjects of his paintings. Ralph even wrote in a letter to me that if Hunter had ever stopped insulting him, he would have known that Hunter had never cared about him "one jot." Ralph explained that most people didn't understand that about Hunter, and those people "looked upon him as a frightening figure consumed with bombast. Or, they tried to appease him, sit in front of the TV with their beers and Chivas Regal to gain his respect." Ralph went on to say that "I have watched teams of total idiots sitting in his bunker with him, swilling away, lowering their voices, hot-damning this and hot-damning that, whooping at the game, but not the content. I think he knew that, but he loved the company like a whore who is desperate to be busy."

Ralph had never spoken like this before, but he always knew where Hunter's heart was: "He was the boss, and tried to tell his friends, 'I am not like the others'—but they never listened, thinking that it was all a game. It *was* a game, of sorts, but the stakes were far higher than they could ever aspire to. It wasn't his weakness; it was theirs."

Now that's wisdom. Like Hunter, Ralph got it in a way few others ever do: Truth really is easier, and honesty truly is the best policy, in any situation.

What Is the Truth?

Hunter's good friend and fellow writer P. J. O'Rourke conducted a series of long, serious, and of course hilarious interviews with him in the 1980s. The last one, in 1987, was originally published in *Rolling Stone*, with the Gonzo portions printed in the inaugural issue of my magazine, *The Woody Creeker*, in February 2006. Hunter explained to P. J. why it is just plain easier to be truthful and why he was such a fan of reality. "Truth is easier," he said, because "you can fall back on the truth. You can't fall back on a story you made up because, by the time [you've finished writing it], you're wondering if it is good or funny or right."

P. J. added that when you at least start with the truth, you can safely embroider upon it. Both Hunter and P. J. were masters of starting with the clean slate of a true story or plain facts and then adding the power of the language to turn it into a brilliant tale—that's the honest truth! Hunter and P. J., although coming from different ends of the political spectrum, shared the love of language as well as the best starting point for any literary journalist: a true story.

Stay True to Your Roots

Hunter always stayed true to his nature, not just as a fun-loving adult adrenaline seeker but all the way back to when he was a smart boy from Louisville, Kentucky, despite the fact that Louisville had branded him as a criminal. One of Hunter's longtime friends and fellow artists, musician David Amram, remembered Hunter as "often shy, sometimes reflective, always witty, and genuinely compassionate." David was one of the artists who performed in Louisville to celebrate "Hunter S. Thompson Day." The auditorium was packed with people from Hunter's past and present, including his mother, Virginia Ray Thompson;

> I like to be the craziest and the sanest person in the room at the same time—either the most hurtful or the most helpful.

his son, Juan; the mayor of Louisville; Johnny Depp; and, of course, Doug Brinkley, all in celebration of Louisville's own Dr. Hunter S. Thompson. The massive gold key that the city gave Hunter that night still hangs in the kitchen here at Owl Farm. Every time I polish it, I thank Louisville for making Hunter such a gentleman, or perhaps I thank Hunter for being such a gentleman despite Louisville's crude treatment of him as a young man. I think every bride should be so lucky as to have a gentleman like

Hunter by her side. The fact that this southern gentleman was also a crazy, gun-toting Gonzo writer made our time together all the more fun.

David Amram remembered that enchanting night in Louisville: "I saw as I listened to him talk that over all the years and through the turmoil of his life, he had somehow kept his roots as a southern gentleman."

The hallmark of any gentleman—or -woman, southern or otherwise—is, of course, integrity, and Hunter remained true all his life to those roots as well. Few writers have ever adhered as closely to Polonius's wise advice to his son Laertes as William Shakespeare phrased it in *Hamlet*: "This above all: to thine own self be true,/And it must follow, as the night the day,/Thou canst not then be false to any man." Bob Braudis assessed Hunter's lifelong commitment to Polonius's axiom in his daily life as well as his profession thusly: "He never wavered. He didn't submit to bullshit. He never gave up his core values, no matter what the cost. And he paid a lot of heavy prices for his steadfastness. But in the end, when you're staring into the grave, are you going to pat yourself on the back for all the wishy-washy adjustments you made or are you going to say, 'Hey, no matter how hard it got, no matter how rough the road, I kept moving'? That's one of the things I prized and prided in Hunter. He never budged from his well-thought-out—always well-thought-out—convictions.

"The opposite of that is compromising," Bob added. "Now I know that he had the ability to compromise when he realized that a lack of flexibility would equal defeat. There were a whole bunch of positions that Hunter would take in his personal life and his professional life that were untenable. Then I would tell him, frankly and with candor, 'Hunter, you're out of your fucking mind. You can't go that way.' And he didn't apologize, he didn't explain, but he definitely changed course … if only to a degree that was within his limits of self-acceptance. To live life on your own terms is something we should all do, and we all—as we come together as tribes and then communities—pick covenants that we agree to abide by for the survival of the community. And Hunter understood that: that a community will not survive unless there are some rules that we all agree to live by." The sheriff gave an example: "One of the categorical imperatives of our society now is as simple as 'When the traffic light is red, stop.'"

In the Belly of the Beast

Hunter was a unique individual. He didn't apologize to anyone for his lifestyle. He even celebrated it. Hal Haddon, Hunter's lead attorney—in the tradition started by Oscar Zeta Acosta in the early 1970s—remembered the first time he met Hunter in person. Hal was Gary Hart's campaign manager and had developed a liking for Hunter's political writing in *Rolling Stone* in the early 1970s. Hal, who had spent the Vietnam years serving as a navy JAG lawyer and, like so many others, had political instincts that took shape in the waning years of the sixties amid the maelstroms of Chicago, Martin Luther King Jr., and Bobby Kennedy, was among the political junkies who ran out to buy every issue of *Rolling Stone* during the 1972 campaign to get his fix of Hunter's political analysis.

After his election to Congress in 1974, Gary Hart wanted to repay his thirty-four-year-old manager somehow, but because the campaign coffers were empty, as they tend to be at the tail end of a political battle, Hal said Gary could pay him by introducing him to Hunter S. Thompson. Gary knew that they would prove a match made in Gonzo heaven, despite their distinctly different lifestyles. Hal is a passionate, powerful criminal lawyer with the straight-shooting style of Abraham Lincoln. He doesn't smoke cigarettes, much less marijuana, and is most definitely not the type of attorney to be found speeding shirtless down the highway à la Oscar Acosta. He has a conservative haircut and, as Gary Hart put it, has a "tall, gangly thing going on," but like Hunter he never apologizes and never explains. Hal, like Hunter, lives his life without the explicit approval of others—and Hal never expressed a need for Hunter's approval either, which is part of the reason he got it so readily. It's no surprise that Hal ended up as Hunter's lead attorney in spite of the marked contrast in their lifestyles.

They had their fateful meeting at the Oxford Hotel in Denver in 1974. Of course Hunter didn't show up for breakfast until four in the afternoon. So Gary Hart and Hunter and Hal spent three hours drinking over a "late breakfast."

"My first impression was absolute awe that this guy could drink three or four Bloody Marys and three or four scotches and sno-cones and a couple of beers and eat huevos rancheros and function," Hal recalled. Most people were awed by such displays of decadence. But what really inspired people was not only that Hunter could live like that, but that he could live like that and not feel the need to apologize to a soul for it.

Hal chuckled at a later memory of his Gonzo client's devotion to the truth, from Hunter's 1991 trial for supposedly assaulting a visiting female porn-industry worker: "When you're a defendant in court, you're supposed to sit there and listen and take it. That really wasn't Hunter's style. So Saskia Jordan, a partner in the law firm, would sit

> I'm creative about getting myself into trouble, so I have to be creative about getting myself out.

on one side of him and [Gerry] Goldstein would sit on the other and whisper at him, write him notes, pull him down, make sure he didn't have whiskey in his water glass; sometimes he did.

"The biggest challenge in representing Hunter was that you'd wake up in the morning and read the daily newspaper and Hunter would have told them what our strategy was. You'd kind of like that to be a surprise. But Hunter, being a journalist, wanted to tell the world what we were going to do in advance. As a lawyer that is just … uncomfortable."

Living Like a Champion

Hunter, like Muhammad Ali, was a champion: a champion of fun and a champion of the underworld, which combined to make him most of all a champion of individualism. As such, he always remained true to his prevailing attitude toward others and the world: take it or leave it. No matter what, he did as he wanted, which wasn't always pleasant for those of us in his orbit.

Hunter was indeed a Lord of the Underworld. I believe it was this dark side, which he celebrated, that made him unique. Not unique in that he had a dark side, because we all do. He was unique in that he embraced rather than ignored that side of himself. It has been said by shamans and yogis that if you ignore your dark side, it will embarrass you. Hunter not only didn't ignore his or try to suppress it, he made a living from it. He once said that it was those dark and ugly instincts that helped him recognize the same in others—particularly those in high places. Senator George McGovern noticed early on that Hunter was always "interested in evil and the concept of evil and wickedness and frequently saw it in high places that other people had learned to live with."

Hunter didn't just celebrate his dark side, he recognized it, seized it, studied it, and magnified it. He was not afraid to shine light in dark places. Richard M. Nixon, for example, was not just despised by Hunter, but endlessly fascinating to him. Hunter didn't just have

If fear is the national currency, then let's have some fun with it.

the pleasure of seeing such wickedness up close and personally; he felt its power in the form of a president. Thus Hunter reaped at least two decades of material for his craft from Nixon. He even admitted that he was left poorer after his favorite nemesis died.

A Road Man for the Lords of Karma

From a very young age, Hunter was observant enough to recognize his own individuality, including that dark side, and was wise enough to learn to do something about it. He didn't try to change his nature; he simply decided to work with the cards that were dealt him. Although he didn't feel that it was necessary to go around preaching the need for others to assert their individuality, he knew that he was going to have to spend the rest of his life expressing his own one way or another, and he understood that he would accomplish more by expressing it on the keys of a typewriter than by letting it express itself in sudden outbursts of frustrated violence.

He even declared in a letter he wrote at age twenty while he was in the air force—and wrote sincerely for the first time in his life—his belief in man as an individual and independent entity: " ... certainly not independence in the everyday sense of the word, but pertaining to a freedom and mobility of thought that few people are able—or even have the courage—to achieve."

Have you ever broken down your own life philosophy? Have you ever thought about the rules that you live by? I asked George McGovern about his. I believe one of the reasons he and Hunter were such great friends and allies was their shared love of the truth. As Senator McGovern put it, "I always try to seek the truth. Sometimes it's hard to find the truth. … But I guess if I were to pull a verse out of biblical wisdom it would be, 'Ye shall know the truth and the truth shall make you free.' So that's been a central factor with me: the quest for truth and then the courage to speak the truth.

"I started off that '72 campaign on a theme that Hunter once told me," George continued. "I said, 'I make one pledge above all others: to seek and speak the truth,' and I did my best to stay with that from beginning to end in that campaign. I'm not so egotistical as to say that I always found the truth. I mean, people have always been searching for the truth. But I did the best I could."

He went on to say that "I always thought

Hunter was in a quest for truth," then added, a bit wistfully, that Hunter "had an idealistic and sentimental side. He really wanted America to be its best, and he wanted politicians to be the best they could be."

It Never Got Weird Enough for Me

"Reality is still stranger than anything I could make up," Hunter said to me one night in May 2002. "I don't know how many years it took to discover that much." This is what Hunter said about the truth when it came to his nemesis, Richard

> Reality is still stranger than anything I could make up.

Nixon. Richard Nixon represented everything that was evil and rotten in the American system. Hunter believed Nixon based his career on lies and corruption to benefit the wealthy few at the expense of the many poor. Until George W. Bush came to power, Hunter believed there was no worse politician in the White House. He wrote in *Better than Sex:* "Some people will say that words like *scum* and *rotten* are wrong for Objective Journalism—which is true, but they miss the point. It was the built-in blind spots of the Objective rules and dogma that allowed Nixon to slither into the White House in the first place. He looked so good on paper that you could almost vote for him sight unseen. He seemed so all-American, so much like Horatio Alger, that he was able to slip through the cracks of Objective Journalism. You had to get Subjective to see Nixon clearly, and the shock of recognition was often painful."

Hunter realized early on in his life that, essentially, he was lazy. This was a curse and a blessing. The curse was that goals were that much harder to reach. But the blessing was that since he knew he would never spend his energies remembering what he said, he decided to always tell the truth, even when it hurts, because in the end, no matter how painful, truth is easier.

LE**SS**ON 6

Buy the Ticket, Take the Ride

Indeed, so I am Lono, as always, and I will always be with you. Always. Never doubt it, never be afraid of anything, no matter how weird it might seem to be, at the time. We are far beyond seems, and we have no Fear … Only moments of Confusion now & then. Ho ho. That will always be our story, our first A.B./H.S.T. creation. We did it, all by our-selves & under some kind of intense deadline pressure in less than two hours' time, from start to finish—from my first desperate flash of a totally fictitious idea to your elegant, fin-ished pages—it was surely the easiest & fast-est and purest piece of high, high *gibberish we had ever written together, until then. The* Lion and the Cadillac. *Stand back and bow down to the Morning Star. Mahalo.*

—Hunter, in a letter to me in March 2003

One thing that Jack Kerouac and Hunter had in common was the understanding of and need for freedom. In the pantheon of American writers, they are perhaps the greatest students and champions of freedom. It is very possible that both decided to become writers not just because they had a talent for it, but because of what the life of a writer, if handled properly, could offer: freedom. Writing is perhaps the only profession you can choose wherein you can live a totally free life and still earn a living; you can go anywhere you want and do or be anything you want, as long as you write about it. Ever since Hunter was a child, he wanted nothing more than freedom—if he had it, everything else in life—fun, love, and nourishment—would fall into place.

He spent his life studying freedom, promoting it, practicing it, and finally writing about it. I believe a large portion of his formative years were spent researching what was necessary to attain freedom. And during that time he had to learn, perhaps the hard way, what to avoid—what is the antifreedom? I think he learned that fear is the antifreedom—because as we gain freedom, which is the opposite of security, we also reap fear. And fear can drive us away from freedom, in a hurry. That, I believe, is why Hunter spent so much of his life fighting fear—and teaching others how to do the same: how to slay that dragon.

His first major study of fear appeared in his first book, *Hell's Angels*, in which Hunter devoted 300 pages to discussing the fear factor and how it gave the Hell's Angels so much power over the public, and how embracing that fear gave the Angels a great deal of freedom. *Fear and Loathing in Las Vegas* is a 300-page argument for freedom in the face of fear. The list goes on, even to Hunter's memoir, *Kingdom of Fear*, a book that cannot be read without realizing that a nation governed by fear can never be truly free.

There is nothing more inhibiting, or more crippling, to freedom than fear. "Needless to say, fear is necessary; imagine if a wild beast had no fear," Hunter once said. And he had it right; fear is necessary, but if gone unchecked, it will make you constantly seek safety, which to Hunter, and perhaps to Kerouac as well as Hemingway and others, is the same as being in prison. "My life is the polar opposite of safe, but I am proud of it," Hunter explained.

Confidence is crucial. He told me so. There is nothing in human life more crippling than fear. Yes, a healthy amount of it is important. But giving it too much importance is unhealthy. Never, ever take yourself too seriously. If you do, you start thinking you have too much to lose, so you start to fear that loss; you lose your freedom. Nowhere was this lesson more apparent than in Hunter's attitude toward his own writing. A close friend and one of Hunter's editors, Jennifer Stroup, recalls, "Every day for Hunter was a warm-up to that hour when he would clear off his typewriter and get ready to work. He always kept the writing—his 'high white note'—in front of him: both the carrot and the reward."

Jack Nicholson fondly remembered his friendship with Hunter, which spanned many decades. The two of them shared a love of the high life of beautiful, smart women, elegant clothes, and utter respect for freedom in the life of an artist. Jack admitted that he wasn't sure if all of us were hypnotized by Hunter as a sort or mad pied piper or not, but he did say that "I know my own children would have been glad to march to any supposed destination for adventure with Hunter … . I would have been more than happy to send them off with Hunter if he thought it was the right thing to do." This statement comes from a responsible, thoughtful parent. I've spent holidays with Jack and his family, before and after Hunter's death, and he always behaved like Father Christmas with his children; he is a very traditional and very good parent. Being willing to send his children off with Hunter to take the ride is a high compliment indeed coming from

Jack. He respected Hunter's professionalism in all things—as Jack wrote in *Rolling Stone*, although Hunter's behavior was provocative, Hunter was after all an expert: an expert at provocation.

Would You Do It Again?

The first documented case of Hunter's study of freedom harks back to when he was just nine years old, when two FBI agents came to his house to question him in a cold, intimidating fashion about a report of a mailbox being tipped over in the path of a speeding bus, sowing terror and confusion among the driver and passengers. The FBI had become involved because the incident involved federal property—a huge green mailbox that Hunter and a group of his young friends had conspired to topple in order to teach their rude substitute bus driver "a lesson."

Before you can feel the first hints of freedom, you need confidence, Hunter explained to me one night. After the boys had successfully performed their nefarious deed, Hunter was back at home reading the sports section. His accomplices were also back home enjoying a routine night with their own families when two grim-looking FBI agents came to the Thompsons' house and terrified Hunter's parents by telling them that their boy was the prime suspect in the case of the toppled mailbox. Because it was a federal offense, it carried a five-year prison sentence. Hunter's mother cried while his father tried in vain to convince the agents that his son was too dumb to understand what he had done.

Because Hunter wasn't even tall enough to reach the top of the mailbox, it was obvious that if he had done it, he had done it with help. The agents went on to say that they had witnesses who had confirmed that Hunter was the culprit. When they presented him the option of ratting out his accomplices to save his own skin, Hunter replied, "What witnesses?" When the flummoxed agents realized that they had been bested by a nine-year-old, they slinked off with a vague and toothless admonition not to do it again—and Hunter learned a lifelong lesson about the importance of facing your fear head-on. Truth, he realized, is not only easier, but also more effective when dealing with bullies, even grown-ups with FBI badges out to prove their toughness.

He would face fear many more times in his life, of course, but that childhood lesson about buying the ticket and taking the ride all the way to the end of the line would stay with him and prove awfully useful for the rest of his life. As he summed the lesson up in "The Lion and Cadillac," it's always better to face your fear—if not directly, then at least by hitting it over the head with a ball-peen hammer from behind. In other words, do whatever works to live your life in the freedom that comes with confronting your fear by beating it senseless and into submission.

Amor Vincit Omnia

I'm not sleepy and there is no place I'm going to.

—*Bob Dylan, "Mr. Tambourine Man," 1964*

After Hunter died, I felt more pain and fear than I knew existed. Suddenly I had lost the safety of being under his wing: no more warm embraces and advice and massive strength to lean on. No more safety. I had the choice of doing exactly what I was told by several family members who came to the surface after his death and suggested that I stay quiet and mind my own business and leave Hunter's legacy to them. "Surely you and Hunter must have been fighting when he died, eh? How can you possibly know what you're doing? ... " "We never really liked ya anyway," I was told. "Be quiet, don't make any waves, and nobody gets hurt" was the message I got. During those dark nights after his death, when I felt very much alone, I realized I would have to make a conscious choice in the face of opposition: would I be crippled by my husband's death, or would I be inspired by his life?

Despite the fact that I was encouraged to "go away," I decided to follow my own instincts and take the path that Hunter and I shared during his life, continuing on with his work as before and sharing what I learned from him with you. And I was met with great opposition. When I requested that Hunter's readers be invited to his funerals, for example, I was told that Hunter's image should never be shared with the masses, be it in *People* magazine or on frivolous blogs. His work, if I truly loved him, I would agree, should be reserved strictly for the few elites who understood the value of his work in "literary history."

I refused to be restricted by that narrow philosophy, and thus am writing this book today. I believe that the more people reading Hunter's work, the better. Every time a young person reads a page of Hunter S. Thompson's, he gains confidence in himself to have courage, and, in my opinion, the world becomes a better place. I have fewer friends in the family because of my belief, and less security as a result, but I bought the ticket when I fell in love with Hunter, and now I'm taking that ride. Instead of discouraging me, it serves to inspire me to dedicate more of my time to spreading his work and philosophy, and to living the Gonzo Way. How funny life can be, eh? In these last paragraphs, I just broke one of the most important rules I learned from Hunter on how to live the Gonzo Way. For the final lesson he taught me is …

LESSON 7

Never Apologize, Never Explain

Res ipsa loquitur.

The End

Acknowledgments

You would not be holding this book if it were not for our beloved senator George McGovern, who introduced me to his editor at Fulcrum Publishing. Out of an interesting conversation over dinner with Sam Scinta, Jeff Kass of the *Rocky Mountain News*, and the senator came the relationship with Fulcrum Publishing that resulted in this book. So thank you, gentlemen.

When I first took on the project, I thought that a shorter book would be easier and more manageable, which I thought was important, as this is my first. But as Blaise Pascal said, "I would have written a shorter letter, but I didn't have the time." Yes, this book has become a much more complex project than I anticipated, and I have many people to thank. Because I wrote it within two years of Hunter's death, a very emotional and turbulent time, many people came together at different stages, and I have them to thank for the completion of this book.

First let me thank my mom, Barbara Siek, for her majestic wisdom and guidance, Shelby Sadler, for her superb editing and weaving of interviews and constant push to keep me writing (and rewriting!), and my beautiful sixteen-year-old niece, Brittany, whom I had in mind while writing every line.

I'd like to thank Doug Brinkley for his friendship and guidance in the Hunter World since the first day I met him, in the kitchen, after he rolled in on a four-wheel-drive bus in the middle of one snowy night. And Ralph Steadman who, in dark and confusing times, when there was no light in sight, started a correspondence with me that provided a desperately needed lifeline. Hal Haddon, who kept the vultures at bay with his Abe Lincoln–like legal peacemaking skills during the creation of this book. George Tobia, for tending the estate financial fires and maintaining the very important business of business. Patricia Blanchet and Ed Bradley, who were friends and allies when I needed them most. Jack Nicholson, who was a good friend during the holiday seasons, and Ann and Michael Owsley, Stacey Hadash, Terry McDonell, and Curtis Robinson, who brought insight and humor into my life during the rough spots. George Stranahan, who developed a community vision oh so many years ago that I benefit from today and that is evident throughout the book. Woody Creek is a gift that he and Patti have given to the entire Gonzo Family. The community of Woody Creek, along with Columbia University, have been the backbone of my support. If you have a solid community, you're home free. And that is my blessing.

And, of course, I extend my deepest gratitude to those friends who gave me their time to be interviewed and talk about their relationships and thoughts on the life and philosophy of my husband, Hunter S. Thompson.

HONOR ROLL

Hunter S. Thompson

Eleanor McGovern

Ed Bradley

Donna Robinson

John Clancy

Tom Benton

David Halberstam

Kurt Vonnegut

David Amram

Jeff Armstrong

Lisl Auman

Ed and Jonathan Bastian

Tom Beach

Marci and Bob Beattie

Alex Bejmuk

Bohdan Bejmuk

Peter Bejmuk

Steve Bennett

Sandra and Porter Bibb

Patricia Blanchet

Bob Braudis

Anne and Doug Brinkley

Phil Bronstein

Sue Carrolan

Graydon Carter

Judy Clancy

Alice Cotton

John Cusack

Louisa Davidson

Morris Dees

Benicio Del Toro

Johnny Depp

Laura Doty

Bob Dylan

Linda and Joe Edwards

Al Eisele

Jennifer and Wayne Ewing

Ben Fee

Tim Ferris

Katie Jo Frank

Joe Fredericks

Cheryl Frymire

Michael Goldberg

Gayle Golding

Lynn Goldsmith

Chris and Gerry Goldstein

Gaylord Guenin

Stacey Hadash

Hal Haddon

Heather Harker

Gary Hart

Josh Hartnett

Bill Havu

Hugh Hefner	Jeff Posternak
Warren Hinckle	Nicki Rapp
Troy Hooper	Manuel Ricco
Stephanie Howard	Keith Richards
Abe Hutt	Curtis Robinson
Jimmy Ibbotson	Rick Rock
Jim Irsay	Rosalind Rosenberg
Emma Juniper	Brittany Ross
Jeff Kass	Lydia Ross
Nicholas Lemann	Zack Ross
Kathleen Lord	Shelby Sadler
Bob Love	Sam Scinta
Lyle Lovett	Chloe Sells
Semmes Luckett	Barbara Siek
Linda Luke	Audrey Sprenger
Faith Marcovecchio	Anna and Ralph Steadman
David McCumber	Tanya and Michael Stepanian
Terry McDonell	Patti and George Stranahan
George McGovern	Jennifer Stroup
Michael Mesnick	Keith Stroup
Tim Mohr	Davison Thompson
Tim Mooney	Robin Thompson
Matt Moseley	Will Thompson
Bill Murray	George Tobia
Jack Nicholson	Torre
Tina and P. J. O'Rourke	John Van Ness
Ann and Michael Owsley	John Walsh
Paul Pascarella	Brandon Wennerd
Sean Penn	Jon Kenneth Williams
Joe Petro	Liz Yount
Julliana and Nancy Pfister	Michael Zilkha